Notes for Coaches:
Continuing professional development

CFM CONSULTING
SERIES ON NOTES FOR COACHES

Notes for Coaches: Continuing professional development

Enabling people to lead the lives they were born to live

PETER HILL

CFM CONSULTING LTD

Consultancy, Coaching and Development

Dunblane · Scotland

Published by CFM Consulting Ltd.
20 Bruce Avenue
Dunblane
Perthshire FK15 9JB
UK
Tel: +44 (0) 1786 821272
Email: peter@cfmconsulting.net
www.coachingformore.co.uk

ISBN:
9780956044709 (paperback)

© CFM Consulting, Limited, 2008

British Library Cataloguing-in-Publication Data.
A catalogue record for this book is available from the British Library.

Book production: Chandos Publishing (Oxford) Ltd. www.chandospublishing.com
Typeset by Domex e-Data Pvt Ltd.
Printed in the UK.

Printed in the UK by 4edge Limited - www.4edge.co.uk

To everyone who worked at, for and with
The Industrial Society during its lifetime

Contents

List of figures and table   *xi*

About the author   *xiii*

Foreword   *xv*

Preface   *xix*

Part 1 – Guide file   **1**

1   Introduction   **3**

    The basic principles   3

    The basic concepts   3

    The key features   4

    CPD is a practical process   4

    The benefits of CPD   5

2   Getting started   **7**

    How adults learn   7

    The learning cycle   9

    Preferred learning styles   10

    Sources of learning   11

3   Preparations   **13**

    Personal stock-take   13

    Defining your objectives   13

    Defining the gap   14

4   Your development plan   **15**

    Why have a plan?   15

    What to include in your plan   15

	Learning contract	16
	Supporting your CPD	16
5	**Recording your CPD**	**17**
	The learning log	17
6	**CPD portfolio**	**19**
	Part 2 – Workbook	**21**
7	**The development checklist**	**23**
	The checklist scoring system	23
	The development checklist	24
8	**Getting started**	**31**
	Learning and learning styles	31
	Learning style information	33
	The 'Practical Learning Styles' package	34
	Honey & Mumford's Learning Styles	35
	Useful information about learning and learning styles	38
	The four modalities	39
	Field-independent vs. field-dependent	40
	Left-brain vs. right-brain	41
	McCarthy's four learning styles	41
	What teaching methods and activities suit different learning styles?	42
	Fifty ways to personal development	44
9	**Preparations**	**47**
	Introducing the Personal Evaluation Tool	47
	The purpose of the Personal Evaluation Tool	47
	How the Personal Evaluation Tool works	48
	Roles and responsibilities	49
	Guidelines on using the Personal Evaluation Tool	51
	Personal stock-take	91

10 The Strategic Evaluation Loop© and sample
    development plans   93
    Identify strategic objectives   93
    Determine learning objectives (ASK)   94
    Define impact targets and objective   95
    Undertake learning   96
    Record impact and transferable learning   96
    Cross-reference impacts to outputs and
    strategic objective   97
    Development plan   99
    Personal development plan to identify CPD needs   100
    Learning contract   101

11 Recording your CPD: learning log and
    development records   103
    Learning log   103
    Ponder session   105
    Development review   106
    Informal learning experiences   106
    Development records   107
    Personal statement   107

Bibliography   109

Index   111

List of figures and table

Figures

1.1 CPD is a practical process 5

2.1 Learning as a consciousness activity 8

2.2 Learning as a planned activity 8

2.3 The learning cycle 9

2.4 Where on the learning cycle do you feel most comfortable? 10

9.1 The Personal Evaluation Wheel 90

10.1 Strategic Evaluation Loop© 94

Table

8.1 The strengths and weaknesses of different learning styles 36

About the author

Peter Hill is the managing director of CFM Consulting Limited and has been working as an executive coach for the past eight years, in the arena of corporate coaching for the past 12 years, and in the field of development and consultancy for the past 18 years.

Peter has been involved with most of the UK's coaching qualifications and has a good overview of the UK coaching scene. He has been instrumental in preparing the groundwork for UK Coaching Standards with the European Coaching and Mentoring Council.

His current portfolio involves clients in Europe, the UK and the USA and he keeps abreast of current trends and developments though his involvement with various bodies and his own continuing professional development through supervision. His major projects include changing the culture at Edinburgh City Council through the coaching and certification of 100 managers through the University of Strathclyde; developing an online coaching competency tool utilising the European Mentoring and Coaching Standards; and developing an approach to supervision within the coaching fraternity for CFM's associates.

He is the author of 'Concepts of Coaching', published by the Institute of Leadership & Management, and produced and features in the Concepts of Coaching DVD, 'GROW'.

Peter uses the person-centred approach to coaching that has been developed in the field of counselling, which allows his clients to develop their own solutions through guided learning.

As a qualified coach from the University of Strathclyde, he is a regular contributor to the national press and media in the UK. He co-founded the School of Coaching at the Industrial Society by managing the Society's approach. He has developed seven UK coaching qualifications at various levels with both the University of Strathclyde and the Institute of Leadership & Management. He is a visiting speaker at the University of Edinburgh Management School on their MBA programme and a teaching practitioner at the University of Strathclyde Business School on their postgraduate certificate in coaching. He is also a qualified master practitioner in neurolinguistic programming. His current research involves an investigation into neural activity when coaching is undertaken.

He is a Fellow of the Institute of Leadership & Management and a Chartered Member of the Chartered Institute of Personnel and Development. He also sits on the Centre for Executive Education Advisory Panel at the University of Strathclyde Business School.

He lives in Dunblane with his wife, two children and a black Labrador dog.

The author can be contacted at:

Tel: +44 (0) 1786 821272
Mobile: +44 (0) 7802 752545
E mail: *peter@cfmconsulting.net*

Foreword

Many years ago, I joined a campaigning organisation called the Industrial Society. They campaigned for better working conditions, better standards, better learning in the workplace, better productivity and a more ethical approach to the world of work. I had learnt my trade in the automotive industry, the fast food environment, and fast-fit tyres and exhausts. Quite a mixture, I grant you, but one of the prerequisites for joining the Society was that you had to have managed people – and I had certainly done that.

I was duly trained and developed not only in the best management theory, but in the heritage of a wonderful organisation. Founded in 1918 by the Reverend Robert Hyde, who introduced basic sanitation to workhouses in the East End of London, the Society had grown from the embryonic campaigns of its founder, through contributing to wartime productivity by introducing 'music while you work' in the munitions factories of the Second World War, through its definitive years in the 1970s and 1980s with John Garnett at the helm, driving leadership (primarily, action-centred leadership) and team briefing – both theories with real practical application. Employment law was campaigned for, education was campaigned for, and indeed, even the homeless were taken into account and lobbied on behalf of.

This was a whole new world for me. So often I had been focused on the bottom line where the 'end nearly always justified the means'. In my heart I was so impressed by the campaigns that, to use another tagline from that era, in my heart 'I bought the company'.

As with most organisations that have a heritage, it must be honoured. Everyone who worked at the Industrial Society did so with heart, spirit and a desire to campaign for a better working life – whether that be working conditions or, in its later stages, leadership, management and development. This book was originally put together by many of the people who worked at, for or with the Industrial Society during its lifetime. Many parts of it were used as continuing professional development by its staff. Much of it was collated by Sheila Marden, Andrew Forrest, Barbara Cohen, Neil Oliver and Jane Mailer, some of whom were even involved in the development of the tools. They are all tools that I have used over the years, either in my own self-development or the development of others through my coaching, mentoring or supervision practice.

I do not claim to be the author of this material, merely the 'sub-editor', and I am keen to ensure that the acknowledgment for as much of the work as possible goes to the right people. I have aimed to source and recognise this appropriately, but if you can assist in this, please get in touch and we will ensure that this is included in future editions. While speaking of acknowledgments, much credit should go to Dr Glyn Jones of Chandos Publishing Ltd for guidance and advice in the whole process, and to Neill Johnstone as the editor who ensured that any idiosyncrasies in my writing were kept at bay and who, with friendly tenacity, kept up the momentum during the approval stage.

The book itself has been put together in this format to assist in the continuing professional development of the people who attend the learning interventions of CFM Consulting Ltd. This could be as delegates, clients, mentees or associates. It is most definitely a 'working book' and not a 'dust collector'. If used wisely it can really enhance your learning.

Peter Hill
Summer 2008

Preface

Welcome to continuing professional development

This guide file and workbook aim to enable you to establish your own programme of continuing professional development.

They provide you with a wide range of practical materials, hints, tips and resources to hep you to cultivate you own development and personal competence.

Continuing professional development (CPD) is an approach to lifelong learning that emphasises self-development. It is based in the belief that we all have enormous untapped potential for learning and development which can be pursued throughout our lives.

- CPD *is systematic, ongoing, self-managed learning.*

- CPD is *continuing* – a person never ceases to learn throughout their life.

- CPD is *professional* – focusing on the personal competencies of the professional.

- CPD is *development* – about improving personal competence, career development and employability.

Part 1
Guide file

Introduction

The basic principles

- Development is *continuous* – the learner actively seeks to improve personal performance.

- Development *is owned and managed* by the learner.

- Effective self-development is personal *and* professional, and starts with the learner's current level of development.

- There are *clear learning objectives* linked to an individual's established development needs.

- Effective self-development requires regular *investment of time*.

- Continuing professional development (CPD) should be seen as an *essential* part of one's life, not as an optional extra.

The basic concepts

- CPD is a flexible approach to individual learning and development.

- Traditional training programmes cannot meet the ongoing development needs of individuals or organisations in a world where change is the norm.

- The development of personal competence is as important as any key knowledge and skills.
- People differ in the ways they learn best. CPD accommodates an individual's preferred learning styles.
- The work environment is a rich source of effective learning from successes and mistakes.
- The value of informal learning is recognised; we all learn by doing.
- While learners take responsibility for their own learning, support may come from a wide range of sources.

The key features

- Defined outcomes.
- A practical plan.
- A balanced mix of activities.
- A development record.
- A record of the learning and how it was applied.

CPD is a practical process

- What do I want/need to learn?
- Why do I want to do this?
- What will I do to achieve this?
- What are the constraints?
- What resources/support will I need?
- What are the critical success criteria?
- What are the target dates?

Figure 1.1 CPD is a practical process

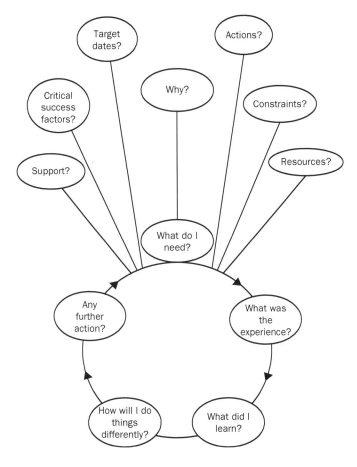

- What did I learn from this activity?
- How will I do things differently?
- Any further action?

The benefits of CPD

- Improved job performance – CPD gives a systematic framework for action to continuously improve personal and professional effectiveness at work.

- Enhanced employability.
- Gaps in present knowledge, skills and attitudes are identified and filled.
- Increased capacity to learn from a wide range of activities.
- Enhanced self-confidence and self-esteem.
- Benefits to the organisation and the team from one's increasing personal competence.
- A more positive attitude to change.
- Able to adopt new ways of working more easily.
- Enables personal growth in a holistic way.

2

Getting started

How adults learn

We are learning all the time, often without realising it. There is no right or wrong way of learning. We are individuals and what matters is that we find the most effective and *enjoyable* way to understand new ideas, learning skills and use information.

As shown in Figure 2.1, there are four main types of *learning*. These are described as:

- *Intuitive*: learning takes place without us being conscious of it.

- *Incidental*: learning is triggered by events which jolt us into thinking about what happened and why.

- *Retrospective*: we make a habit of thinking about activities and events and analysing what we have learned from them.

- *Prospective*: we plan to learn from before an experience as well as reviewing it afterwards.

Effective learning happens when:

- it is a conscious/deliberate activity; *and*
- it is carefully planned.

Figure 2.1 Learning as a consciousness activity

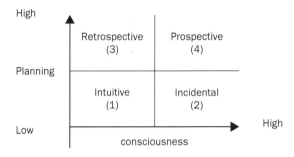

There are four types of *learner* (Figure 2.2)

- *Sleepers* are intuitive and show little initiative or response to their experiences.

- *Adventurers* respond to and learn from opportunities that come their way, but tend not to create opportunities for themselves.

- *Warriors* plan experiences but tend not to learn from them.

- *Sages* both plan and learn from their experience.

Figure 2.2 Learning as a planned activity

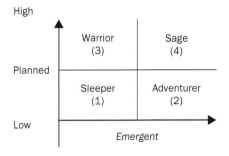

In *Cultivating Self Development*, Megginson and Whitaker (1996) develop the concepts of *planned learning* and *emergent learning*. Learners with the former approach take responsibility for the direction of their learning, while learners with the latter approach respond to and learn from their experiences.

Finally, Sylvia Downs (1995) uses the MUD acronym to describe the three kinds of learnings:

- M: Memorising, e.g. multiplication tables;

- U: Understanding, e.g. why the sun rises and sets;

- D: Doing, e.g. driving, cookery, first aid.

The learning cycle

Effective learning consists of the four *linked* stages of the learning cycle (Figure 2.3).Thus, the essence of effective CPD is not the experience itself, but the *actual learning outcome*:

- *Reviewing*: Thinking about what happened and why.

- *Concluding*: Placing experience in context and deciding the validity and relevance of what has been learned.

- *Planning*: What will I do differently as a result of this experience? Any further actions?

Figure 2.3 The learning cycle

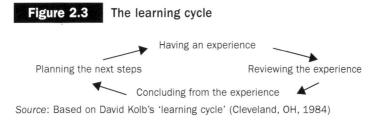

Source: Based on David Kolb's 'learning cycle' (Cleveland, OH, 1984)

Preferred learning styles

It is a common experience that if two people with the same needs are given the same learning activity, one will learn a lot, the other only a little. In the same way, just as some individuals have a preference for one learning style, so some learning activities are strongly geared to one style of learning.

Peter Honey and Alan Mumford (2006) have adapted the learning cycle to identify four learning styles (Figure 2.4). It is interesting to try to match these with the other four main types of learning described above:

- activist – intuitive/incidental;
- reflector – retrospective;
- theorist – retrospective/prospective;
- pragmatist – prospective, if linked to practical goals.

Figure 2.4   **Where on the learning cycle do you feel most comfortable?**

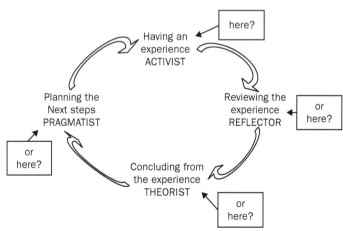

Are you prone to:
rushing around keeping busy? analysing things to death? jumping to conclusions? quick fixes?

Source: Peter Honey Publications.

To discover how to identify and develop your learning styles, see Honey and Mumford's Learning Styles Questionnaire at *www.peterhoney.com*. The questionnaire will reveal all and show you how to become a more effective learner (it will only take ten minutes to complete and another five minutes to score/interpret). It is totally non-threatening – there are no right or wrong answers, anyone can do it and it is easy to understand.

Honey and Mumford's Learning Styles Questionnaire will help you find out:

- how to fire on all four learning cylinders (use them, or lose them!); and

- how to choose learning methods that suit your style (horses for courses!)

Sources of learning

Sources of learning include:

- work-based;

- personal activities outside work;

- courses, seminars, conferences;

- self-managed and informal learning;

- working with a coach or mentor.

See: 'Fifty ways to personal development' in the workbook.

Preparations

Personal stock-take

Audit current skills, knowledge, attitudes and personal competencies, experience, qualifications and achievements against needs/goals and how others see you (through feedback from coach, mentor or colleagues).

Tools include:

- SWOT analysis;
- personal evaluation tool;
- 360-degree appraisal/feedback;
- competencies;
- the development checklist;
- MCI standards;
- five-way management;
- appraisal;
- feedback from questionnaires.

Defining your objectives

Tools include:

- GROW model;
- SMART objectives;

- checklists;
- coaching or mentoring conversations.

Defining the gap

Recognising the gap between what is needed/desired and the current situation as described in the findings of the personal stock-take:

closing the gap = the goal to be accomplished.

Your development plan

Why have a plan?

A plan is important for a systematic and disciplined approach to one's learning and development. It should ask:

- What do I want to do?
- Why do I want to do this?
- What do I hope this activity will achieve?
- How will I know when I'm getting there?

What to include in your plan

Your plan should include:

- the identified learning needs;
- the learning objectives defined;
- the design of the learning process;
- any constraints;
- the resources/support required;
- the critical success criteria;
- timescale and way marks.

Learning contract

The learning contract is a formal way of committing to the plan, particularly when some form of personal support is involved.

Supporting your CPD

Support for your continuing professional development might come from some of the following:

- your line manager;
- a trusted colleague;
- trusted staff;
- friends;
- mentor;
- coach;
- learning facilitator;
- speaking partner;
- a learning set.

5

Recording your CPD

The learning log

The learning log is a key tool for deepening individual learning. It records:

- development plans/agreements;

- nominal/notional learning hours;

- development records;

- reviews of experiences – ensure you describe what actually happened in some detail;

- any conclusions from the experience – these are your learning points;

- planning for the next steps – decide which action points you wish to implement and work out an action plan, i.e. what you are going to do and how and when you are going to do it;

- ponder sessions – follow the same steps as those described above – it is all about the application of the learning and answering the question: what are you going to do differently as a result of this experience?

6

CPD portfolio

What to include in your portfolio:

- who you are and what you do;
- your accomplishments – hobbies, qualifications, special skills or abilities;
- assessment results;
- personal stock-take;
- your development plan;
- your learning log;
- development records;
- personal statements.

Sample formats for all the items suggested above can be found in the workbook.

Once established, your portfolio will grow and develop with you. As it will serve many purposes in your future personal and professional life, your portfolio should reflect the whole of you and your personality in the context of your life and work.

A wide variety of media may be used, including photographs, documents, samples of work, DVDs, audio CDs, records of achievement and published work.

Enjoy portraying yourself as imaginatively and creatively as you can – have fun!

Part 2
Workbook

7

The development checklist

The most important part of a development programme lies in achieving your own personal objectives. To do this you need to be clear about what you want from the programme. The development checklist will help you quantify your development needs and formulate some objectives.

The checklist covers the following areas:

- managing yourself;

- managing your job;

- managing people;

- managing your environment;

- managing your specialist function.

The checklist scoring system

The importance or relevance of the topics will vary according to the nature of your job. The levels of your present knowledge, skills and competence will also vary:

- *Relevance in your job*: Score 3 for high (H), 2 for medium (M), and 1 for low (L) levels of skill or competence.

- *Level of skill*: Score 1 for high (H), 2 for medium (M), and 3 for low (L) levels of skill or competence.

- *Learning need*: Multiply the *relevance* score by the *skill* score for an early indication of your learning need priorities (9 = top priority).
- *Your development plan*: Your coach, mentor, manager or team leader will help you to draw up your plan, based on your learning needs.

This will become a rolling programme of development as objectives are achieved and new ones arise.

The development checklist

Manage yourself

	Relevance in your job H = 3 M = 2 L = 1	Level of skill H = 3 M = 2 L = 1	Priority learning needs
Manage your time identify key activities set priorities delegate work avoid time-wasting activities			
Manage stress cope with pressures recognise personal stress			
Manage your career seek to achieve personal objectives seek to achieve organisational objectives keep yourself up to date			

Manage your job

	Relevance in your job	Level of skill	Priority learning needs
Forecast events and requirements			
awareness of your environment			
anticipate the future			
identify impacts on your department			
Plan for the future			
adopt suitable planning techniques			
create schedules for activities			
assess requirements			
Set objectives			
interpret directives and objectives from higher authorities			
set departmental objectives			
set personal objective			
Exercise control (over output, performance, quality)			
establish standards			
establish systems to monitor performance against agreed standards			
take appropriate action to correct discrepancies			
Manage resources			
establish budgets			
operate budgets			
manage use of equipment			
manage use of facilities			
manage use of buildings etc			

	Relevance in your job	Level of skill	Priority learning needs
Deal with opportunities and problems			
identify issues			
assemble information			
generate possible solutions			
evaluate solutions			
take decisions			
plan for uncertainty			
set controls and feedback			
establish procedures and routines			
practise accountability			
delegate work			
clarify responsibility			
grant authority			
establish reporting requirements			

Manage people

	Relevance in your job	Level of skill	Priority learning needs
Select people			
determine job requirements			
write job descriptions			
prepare personnel specifications			
write job advertisements			
plan selection interviews			
conduct/participate in selection interviews			
match people to jobs/ jobs to people			
Lead people			
build teams			

	Relevance in your job	Level of skill	Priority learning needs
seek to improve performance, output, productivity			
motivate people			
design appropriate structures			
Develop people			
assess performances			
appraise people's needs			
counsel them			
coach them			
train them			
provide opportunities			
be supportive			
Exercise discipline			
set (or adopt) standards			
monitor performances and behaviours			
follow disciplinary procedures			
conduct disciplinary interviews			
Handle conflict			
deal with grievances			
identify causes of conflict			
seek to harmonise			
exercise power and authority in an appropriate manner			
Communicate with people			
seek information from people			
seek to inform people (notify, report, tell, teach)			
seek to influence (persuade, convince)			

	Relevance in your job	Level of skill	Priority learning needs

in writing:
   – correspondence
   – reports
   – papers
 in speech
   – briefings
   – presentations
   – negotiations
   – interviews
   – counselling
   – teaching
 chair meetings
 conduct and participate in meetings
 Establish relationships
 build networks
 build appliances with support			

Manage your environment

	Relevance in your job	Level of skill	Priority learning needs
Take account of organisational influences organisational objectives organisational constraints organisational norms organisational culture organisational politics *Recognise and cope with organisational related topics* boundary frictions conflicting demands incongruent objectives			

	Relevance in your job	Level of skill	Priority learning needs
conflicting perspectives			
different timescales			
different cultures, languages, values			
unsuitable structures			
unclear responsibilities			
inadequate communication flows			
needed developments and improvements in your organisation			
the organisational 'tone' of your department			
needed standards and reforms			
necessary changes in management style			
Take account of factors outside the organisation			
the supremacy of the client/customer			
the law			
the economy			
technological developments			
sociological trends			
demography			
government			
Manage change			
cope with imposed change			
initiate changes in your organisation			
plan for change			
identify and take account of the impact of change			
apply change management techniques			

Manage your specialist function

	Relevance in your job	Level of skill	Priority learning needs
Apply specialised techniques and professional knowledge			

8

Getting started

All the questionnaires listed below explore specific areas of competence you might like to develop:

- Belbin's Team Role Inventory® (available from *www .belbin.com*)
- Coaching Competencies Assessment Questionnaire*
- Honey & Mumford's Learning Styles Questionnaire® (available from *www.peterhoney.com*)
- Practical Learning Styles Questionnaire®*
- Margerison-McCann Team Management Development® (available from *www.tmsdi.co.uk*)
- Myers Briggs Type Indicator® (available from *www.opp .eu.com*)
- Personal Evaluation Tool* (included)

*Available from CFM Consulting Ltd (*http://www.coachingformore .co.uk*)

Learning and learning styles

It is widely accepted that not everyone learns and processes information in the same way. Given the same learning opportunity, two people will most likely want very different things to enable them to learn effectively. Accordingly, it is possible to become a more effective learner and coach if you have a better understanding of want you need from a learning experience, or how the client learns.

Karen Tidswell and Keith Rogers (1998) have designed a package entitled 'Practical Learning Styles' to identify what each individual needs as a learner. In particular it assesses:

- the way you prefer information to be presented;
- the way you prefer to make sense of information.

The 'Practical Learning Styles' Questionnaire is designed to identify learning preferences according to four dimensions. Each dimension has an associated pair of learning styles as described below:

- *Orientation*: This focuses on your instructional preference and assesses whether you are a *realistic* or a *creative* learner. Typically, a realistic learner prefers practical courses and likes to learn in small connected chunks, whereas a creative learner prefers imaginative courses and gains understanding in large holistic leaps.

- *Interaction*: This focuses on your approach to study and assesses whether you are a *doer* or a *thinker*. Typically, a doer likes activity-based learning, whereas a thinker likes time to reflect and plan learning.

- *Representation*: This focuses on your mental representation of material to be learned and assesses whether you are a *verbaliser* or a *visualiser*. Typically, a verbaliser presents and learns information using words, whereas a visualiser prefers to use images and diagrams.

- *Processing*: This focuses on the learning process you use to remember new information and assesses whether you are a *surface* or a *deep processor*. Typically, a surface processor likes to learn by rote, whereas a deep processor likes to understand underlying concepts.

Learning style information

Outlined below is a summary of the learning style information for each dimension, including the differences between the extremes for each pair of learning styles and what the extremes prefer.

Realistic – Creative

This dimension focuses on your *instructional preference* and assesses whether your preferred learning style is that of a *realistic* or *creative* learner. It assesses what kind of data you prefer to learn with – in other words whether you prefer practical or creative courses. This dimension considers whether or not you prefer to:

- concentrate on one thing at a time in order to develop a depth of understanding;
- work on several things at once in order to develop a breadth of understanding.

Doer – Thinker

This dimension focuses on your *approach to study* and assesses whether your preferred learning style is that of a *doer* or a *thinker*. It assesses whether you:

- like action and variety in your learning experiences;
- prefer time alone for reflection and contemplation;
- like learning with others or alone.

Verbaliser – Visualiser

This dimension focuses on your *mental representation* of the material to be learned and assesses whether your preferred learning style is that of a *verbaliser* or a *visualiser*. This dimension determines whether you prefer material to be presented to you in pictures, images and diagrams, or whether you prefer the written word to be used. Everyone can use both modes of representation but most people have a defined preference for one over the other.

Surface processor – Deep processor

This dimension focuses on the *learning process* that you use to remember new information and assesses whether your preferred learning style is that of a *surface* or a *deep processor*. It determines whether you prefer to learn by memorising facts or by understanding underlying concepts. It examines whether you learn best by using rote learning techniques or by reinterpreting new information in your own words. It also determines whether you learn just enough to get by, or whether you actually enjoy delving deeper than is necessary into new subjects.

The 'Practical Learning Styles' package

Through completing the 'Practical Learning Styles' package, it is possible to identify your learning preferences. Also it provides greater understanding of the meaning of these preferences and thus enables you to develop your learning style to become a more balanced and flexible learner. Furthermore, by establishing your own learning style preferences and undertaking the associated development activities, you will be able to tackle new learning tasks with greater efficiency and effectiveness. With that knowledge, from a coach's perspective, you can couch the language you use in terms that make it easier for your client to understand and learn.

The Practical Learning Styles Package can be purchased from *http://www.coachingformore.co.uk/shop*.

Honey & Mumford's Learning Styles

This is a much-used learning styles assessment in the world of work. Once again, by taking a simple questionnaire, you can ascertain your preferences. They are divided into the four key areas outlined below and summarised in Table 8.1. The Honey and Mumford Learning Styles assessment tool is available from *www.peterhoney.com*.

Activists

Activists involve themselves fully and without bias in new experiences. They enjoy the here and now and are happy to be dominated by immediate experiences. They are open-minded, not sceptical, and this tends to make them enthusiastic about anything new. Their philosophy is 'I'll try anything once'. They tend to act first and consider the consequences afterwards. Their days are filled with activity. They tackle problems by brainstorming. As soon as the excitement from one activity has died down they are busy looking for the next. They tend to thrive on the challenge of new experiences, but are bored with implementation and longer-term consolidation. They are gregarious people, constantly involving themselves with others but, in doing so, they seek to focus all activities on themselves.

Table 8.1 The strengths and weaknesses of different learning styles

Strengths	Weaknesses
Activists Flexible and open-minded Happy to have a go Happy to be exposed to new situations Optimistic about anything new and therefore unlikely to resist change	Tendency to take the immediately obvious action with thinking Often take unnecessary risks Tendency to do too much themselves and hog the limelight Rush into action with insufficient preparation Get bored with implementation/consolidation
Reflector Careful Thorough and methodical Thoughtful Good at listening to others and assimilating information Rarely jumps to conclusions	Tendency to hold back from direct participation Slow to make up their minds and reach a decision Tendency to be too cautious and not take enough risks Not assertive – they are not particularly forthcoming and have no 'small talk'
Theorist Logical 'vertical' thinkers Rational and objective Good at asking probing questions Disciplined approach	Restricted in lateral thinking Low tolerance for uncertainty, disorder and ambiguity Intolerant of anything subjective or intuitive Full of 'shoulds, oughts and musts'
Pragmatist Keen to test things out in practice Practical, down to earth, realistic Businesslike – gets straight to the point Technique-oriented	Tendency to reject anything without an obvious applications Not very interested in theory or basic principles Tendency to seize on the first expedient solution to a problem Impatient with waffle On balance, task-oriented not people-oriented

Reflectors

Reflectors like to stand back to ponder experiences and observe them from many different perspectives. They collect data, both first-hand and from others, and prefer to think about things thoroughly before coming to any conclusions. The thorough collection and analysis of data about experiences and events is what counts, so they tend to postpone definite conclusions for as long as possible. Their philosophy is to be cautious. They are thoughtful people who like to consider all possible angles and implications before making a move. They prefer to take a back seat in meetings and discussions. They enjoy observing other people in action. They listen to others and get the drift of the discussion before making their own points. They tend to adopt a low profile and have a slightly distant, tolerant, unruffled air about them. When they act it is part of a wide picture which includes the past as well as the present and others' observations as well as their own.

Theorists

Theorists adapt and integrate observations into complex but logically sound theories. They think problems through in a logical, step-by-step way. They assimilate disparate facts into coherent theories. They tend to be perfectionists who won't rest easy until things are tidy and fit into a rational scheme. They like to analyse and synthesise. They are keen on basic assumptions, principles, theories models and systems thinking. Their philosophy prizes rationality and logic: 'If it's logical it's good'. Questions they frequently ask are: 'Does it make sense?' 'How does this fit with that?' 'What are the basic assumptions?' They tend to be detached, analytical and dedicated to rational objectivity rather than anything subjective or ambiguous. Their approach to problems is consistently logical. This is their 'mental set', and they rigidly reject anything that doesn't fit with it. They prefer to maximise certainty and feel uncomfortable with subjective judgments, lateral thinking and anything flippant.

Pragmatists

Pragmatists are keen on trying out ideas, theories and techniques to see if they work in practice. They positively search out new ideas and take the first opportunity to experiment with applications. They are the sort of people who return from management courses brimming with new ideas that they want to try out in practice. They tend to be impatient with ruminating and open-ended discussions. They are essentially practical, down-to-earth people who like making practical decisions and solving problems. They respond to problems and opportunities 'as a challenge'. Their philosophy is: 'There is always a better way', and 'If it *works* it is good'.

Useful information about learning and learning styles

Learners will be more successful if you match your teaching style to their learning styles. Cheron Verster, teacher trainer and materials developer from South Africa, offers the following guidance on learning styles. You may find this useful in your reflections on your learning and your teaching or coaching.

- *What is a learning style?* Ellis (1985) describes a learning style as the more or less consistent way in which a person perceives, conceptualises, organises and recalls information.

- *Where do learning styles come from?* Your learners' learning styles will be influenced by their genetic make-up, their previous learning experiences, their culture and the society in which they live.

- *Why should teachers know about learning styles?* Sue Davidoff and Owen van den Berg (1990) suggest four steps: plan, teach/act, observe and reflect. Here are some guidelines for each step.

  - Learners learn better and more quickly if the teaching methods used match their preferred learning styles.

  - As learning improves, so too does self-esteem. This has a further positive effect on learning.

  - Learners who have become bored with learning may become interested once again.

  - The student–teacher relationship can improve because the student is more successful and is more interested in learning.

- *What types of learning styles are there?* There are many ways of looking at learning styles. Some of the classification systems that researchers have developed are explored below.

The four modalities

This work originates from that of Drs Bandler and Grinder in the field of neurolinguistic programming (see *www.richardbandler.com* and *www.nlpu.com/grindbio.htm*). Their work suggests that learners may prefer a visual (seeing), auditory (hearing), kinaesthetic (moving) or tactile (touching) way of learning:

- Those who prefer a visual learning style:
  - look at the teacher's face intently;
  - like looking at wall displays, books and the like;
  - often recognise words by sight;

- use lists to organise their thoughts;
- recall information by remembering how it was set out on a page.

■ Those who prefer an auditory learning style:
  - like the teacher to provide verbal instructions;
  - like dialogues, discussions and plays;
  - solve problems by talking about them;
  - use rhythm and sound as memory aids.

■ Those who prefer a kinaesthetic learning style:
  - learn best when they are involved or active;
  - find it difficult to sit still for long periods;
  - use movement as a memory aid.

■ Those who prefer a tactile way of learning:
  - use writing and drawing as memory aids.
  - learn well in hands-on activities like projects and demonstrations.

Field-independent vs. field-dependent

Field-independent learners

Field-independent learners can easily separate important details from a complex or confusing background. They tend to rely on themselves and their own thought-system when solving problems. They are not so skilled in interpersonal relationships.

Field-dependent learners

Field-dependent learners find it more difficult to see the parts in a complex whole. They rely on others' ideas when solving problems and are good at interpersonal relationships.

Left-brain vs. right-brain

Learners who are left-brain dominated:

- are intellectual;
- process information in a linear way;
- tend to be objective;
- prefer established, certain information;
- rely on language in thinking and remembering.

Those who are right-brain dominated:

- are intuitive;
- process information in a holistic way;
- tend to be subjective;
- prefer elusive, uncertain information;
- rely on drawing and manipulating to help them think and learn.

McCarthy's four learning styles

McCarthy (1980) described learners as innovative learners, analytic learners, commonsense learners or dynamic learners:

- Innovative learners:
  - look for personal meaning while learning;
  - draw on their values, opinions and beliefs while learning;
  - enjoy social interaction;
  - are cooperative and have to make forced value, not necessarily practical application judgments.
- Analytic learners:
  - want to develop intellectually while learning;

- draw on facts while learning;
- are patient and reflective;
- want to know 'important things' and to add to the world's knowledge.
- Commonsense learners:
  - want to find solutions and use problem-solving activities;
  - value things if they are useful;
  - are kinaesthetic;
  - are practical and straightforward;
  - want to make things happen.
- Dynamic learners:
  - look for hidden possibilities;
  - judge things by gut reactions;
  - synthesise information from different sources;
  - are enthusiastic and adventurous and use a variety of challenging activities;
  - Work best when asked about their feelings.

What teaching methods and activities suit different learning styles?

If you vary the activities that you use in your learning, you will add breadth as well as depth to your learning.

The four modalities of teaching

- Visual:
  - use many visuals in the classroom. For example, wall displays posters, flash cards, graphic organisers etc.

- Auditory:
  - use audio CDs and videos, storytelling, songs, jazz chants, memorisation and drills;
  - allow learners to work in pairs and small groups regularly.
- Kinaesthetic:
  - use physical activities, competitions, board games, role plays and the like;
  - intersperse activities which require learners to sit quietly with activities that allow them to move around and be active.
- Tactile:
  - use board and card games, demonstrations, projects, role plays and the like;
  - use 'while-listening' and reading activities; for example, ask learners to fill in a table while listening to a talk, or to label a diagram while reading.

Field-independent vs. field-dependent

- *Field-independent*: let learners work on some activities on their own.
- *Field-dependent*: let learners work on some activities in pairs and small groups.

Left-brain vs. right-brain dominated

- Left-brain dominated:
  - give verbal instructions and explanations;
  - set some closed tasks to which learners can discover the 'right' answer.

- Right-brained dominated:
  - write instructions as well as giving them verbally;
  - demonstrate what you would like learners to do;
  - give learners clear guidelines, a structure, for tasks;
  - set some open-ended tasks for which there is no 'right' answer;
  - sometimes allow learners to respond by drawing.

Fifty ways to personal development

Choose from these 50 activities to help achieve your personal and professional potential. From Andrew Forrest (Industrial Society, 1994).

Individual learning

1. Develop your learning skills
2. Try guided reading
3. Write a report summary or book review
4. Keep a learning log
5. Listen to CDs 'on the move'
6. Try computer-based learning
7. Study for a professional qualification
8. Undertake an open learning programme
9. Gain an NVQ

Group work

10. Visit other organisations
11. Action learning

12. 'Adopt' a company

13. Serve on a task force or working party

14. Participate in a business game or simulation

15. Self-managed learning

16. Outdoors training

17. Attend a training course

Change of duties

18. Undertake a secondment to another organisation

19. Take up office in the community

20. Undertake a secondment or 'job swap' within your organisation

21. Undertake a sabbatical

22. Carry out a short project attachment to another organisation

23. Work shadowing

24. Act as a non-executive director

25. Deputise for your manager

26. Take on new responsibilities

Represent your organisation or your colleagues

27. Represent your organisation or profession

28. Serve as a staff representative or shop steward

29. Serve an education/industry link organisation

30. Work on a community project

Respond to guidance

31. Respond to guidance from your immediate manager
32. Accept newly delegate responsibility
33. Respond to all-round feedback
34. Use guidance from a mentor
35. Identify a manager who is excellent at developing people
36. Use diagnostic instruments

Creative skills

37. Carry out a constructive 'post mortem' on a success or failure
38. Use the Strategic Evaluation Loop© (p. 93)
39. Change the way you tackle your work
40. Use each inspection as a learning opportunity
41. Write a major report
42. Analyse the actions of effective leaders
43. Take part in a debate
44. Benchmarking

Building up contacts

45. Join a user group
46. Actively participate in your professional body
47. Develop a network
48. Join a support group

Develop others

49. Coach your own staff
50. Delegate part of your job

9

Preparations

Introducing the Personal Evaluation Tool

The Personal Evaluation Tool (PET) is a unique approach to helping people self-evaluate their skills and abilities in working with others. The PET is made up of 12 ability areas which are key to working effectively with others.

The purpose of the Personal Evaluation Tool

The purpose of the PET is to help individuals generate a precise evaluation of their abilities when working with others, which can be used as a starting point for further discussion and action.

The context within which the PET is applied is unique to each individual user; therefore, to gain maximum benefit, the user must first be clear why they want to use it. This need may be identified in a number of ways, for example:

- at a one-to-one discussion between the potential user and their line manager;
- as an outcome of an annual review;
- as part of a mentoring relationship;
- as the start of a coaching conversation.

Listed below are examples of where the PET could be used:

- when boundaries of a present job change;
- to help create a more focused personal development plan;
- in preparation for taking up a new post;
- assessing present abilities before making career decisions;
- as part of reviewing difficulties or frustrations at work;
- return to work (e.g. sickness, maternity leave);
- purely to explore how you are doing;
- to build better and more productive relationships with people at work;
- to be a more effective member/leader of a project team.

How the Personal Evaluation Tool works

Once the need has been identified and the user is clear of the context in which they are going to apply the PET, there are three stages to the process.

Stage one

Self-evaluation of ability areas

The PET is made up of 12 ability areas which are key to working effectively with others. Each area has nine or ten statements reflecting a different level of ability. After carefully reading through each statement the user circles the statement that they believe best reflects their current level of ability.

When all 12 abilities have been completed, the result are plotted onto the Personal Evaluation Wheel (Figure 9.1).

Stage two

The Personal Evaluation Wheel

This gives the user a visual representation of their evaluation, which can aid the discussion at stage three.

Stage three

Discussion of the evaluation

The user owns their evaluation results and should decide how best they can use them, not forgetting the context within which the PET was originally completed. There needs to be commitment to taking action on those results from which the user will most benefit. To aid this process, the system has been designed to include at least one one-to-one session with a PET supporter, coach or mentor. However, the user may prefer to review the results themselves.

> 'The use of the self-analysis questionnaire was most valuable in getting me to stop and think about how I operate.' (Ian Lawson, Campaign for Leadership Director, The Industrial Society)

Roles and responsibilities

The user, the supporter, and the line manager, all have an important role to play in the PET process. The user's relationship with their supporter is relatively short – a maximum of three one-to-one sessions, whereas the relationship with their line manager is ongoing. It is important therefore, that the user considers how best to keep their line manager informed of the outcomes of supporter sessions, and what impact these may have on their future role and development.

The supporter, coach or mentor

The supporter's role is to assist the user to gain maximum benefit from the evaluation and thus achieve the desired outcomes. Their responsibilities include:

- assisting the user to gain a full understanding of their results, within the context it was completed;
- giving encouragement to the user to develop an action plan;
- respecting the confidentiality of the one-to-ones.

The user

The user's role is an active one. It is the user's responsibility to identify the context within which they wish to use the PET, and to focus on possible outcomes. To get the most out of their evaluation the user should:

- explain to their supporter the context in which the PET was completed;
- be open and honest in their discussions with their supporter;
- focus on commitment to action and progressing important findings.

At all times the user must respect the confidential aspects of the one-to-one sessions.

The line manager

The line manager must fulfil the responsibilities they have for developing their staff, which include:

- on-the-job support;
- feedback on work performance;
- performance review;
- continuous improvement.

It is important for the line manager to respect the confidentiality of the one-to-one sessions between the user and supporter and view the tool for what it is – an additional aid to the development of a member of staff. However, the line manager should also ensure that they give the user, if they so choose, plenty of opportunities to discuss the outcomes of the sessions.

Guidelines on using the Personal Evaluation Tool

How do I complete the PET?

First read the following instructions carefully. If you have any difficulties in understanding exactly what you need to do contact Peter Hill at *http://www.coachingformore.co.uk*.

- Read the one-line description of the particular ability area. Make sure you understand its meaning before reading the first statement.
- Ask yourself 'does this statement express the total extent of my ability regarding this issue?'

- If your answer indicates that you feel that you might have a greater level of ability, then move on to the second statement and ask the same question.

- Continue through the statements in order (do not jump statements) until you reach the one that you feel expresses the real level of your present ability.

- Stop and circle the number of this statement.

- Check the next statement to confirm that your initial judgment was correct.

- Where possible, write a sentence or two at the bottom of the page giving reasons for your choice and, if appropriate, record any commitments or possible actions in the space provided.

- Move on to the next skill area.

Important: Do not see a 'stop' early on in any key ability as a failure. There could be valid reasons for this result, some of which have nothing to do with you.

Possible 'what ifs'

What if I am unsure and I think I am somewhere between '5' and '6'.

If you feel you are somewhere between two following statements, circle both statements and write between them a description of your level of ability.

What if I don't understand the meaning of certain phrases used?

At the end of each ability area is a section called 'Guide to meaning of terms'. The section includes definitions for those phrases which have been asterisked in the text.

What if none of the statements really reflects my level?

If you become completely stuck and cannot reach a decision, write a description which you feel states your level of ability in the space at the end of the section.

What do I do when I have worked through all 12 ability areas?

First, plot them on the Personal Evaluation Wheel. Then contact your supporter to arrange a meeting where you can discuss the results. Remember, the PET is designed to include at least one one-to-one session. Maximum benefit usually comes through the individual/supporter partnership. However, if you prefer, you could talk through the results with your line manager or look through them on your own, reviewing your results against the needs of your job.

Finally, any results are yours. You decide how you will use them. However, do not forget your original focus and context in completing the PET. Give commitment to actioning the results where you can see the benefit.

Important: at any stage, please feel free to contact your supporter or Peter Hill at *http://www.coachingformore.co.uk*.

Problem solving

Having a commitment to solve problems through full understanding and most effective use of human and/or other resources.

1. I generally only recognise problems that are within my past experience.

2. I am quite good at recognising simple problems,* but have difficulty finding answers.

3. I am good at solving simple problems but only with the help of others.

4. I am confident in my ability to identify and solve simple problems with or without the help of others.

5. I recognise the more complex problems,* but have difficulty finding effective solutions.

6. I can recognise and solve complex problems as long as I have the support of others.

7. I take responsibility for solving complex problems, with or without involving others.

8. I am often able to identify major problems,* even in complex situations. Where appropriate I involve others in finding effective solutions.

9. I am always able to understand major problems, even in complex situations. I rapidly develop effective solutions through the involvement of others, or the use of resources.

Please remember you may score between the numbers.

Space is provided for you to make comments to describe your personal level of effectiveness. You may find it useful to make notes as this might assist you in your discussions with your supporter.

Guide to meaning of terms

'*Simple problem*', easy to understand: e.g. getting an important message to someone off site.

'*Complex problem*', made up of many interconnected issues: e.g. involving several people in reaching an agreement on a contentious issue.

'*Major problem*', made up of many interconnected issues of great importance/priority or significance: e.g. handling a customer complaint satisfactorily.

Comments and actions

Please add extra sheets if you need more space for your notes.

Comments

Actions

To be completed during your discussions with your supporter.

Growing others

Using facilitation skills to enable others to develop their knowledge skills or confidence.

1. I don't believe I have a responsibility to help others with their growth and development.

2. I do not have the opportunity to help other people with their growth and development at work.

3. I have the opportunity to help my immediate colleagues* to develop,* but I do not have the skills or knowledge.

4. I occasionally help my immediate colleagues to develop but I do not have confidence in my skills.

5. I am confident about using my skills to develop my immediate colleagues at work.

6. I use my skills unconsciously to help develop my immediate colleagues at work. I do not have the opportunity to develop other people at work.

7. I use my skills unconsciously to help develop my immediate colleagues at work. I would not use this skill to develop other people at work even if the opportunity arose.

8. When I feel comfortable with the person and the subject, I am confident about using my skills to help develop people at work.

9. Regardless of the person or subject, I do all I can to assist anyone at work to take responsibility to reach their full potential.

Please remember you may score between numbers.

Space is provided for you to make comments to describe your personal level of effectiveness. You may find it useful to make notes as this might assist you in your discussions with your supporter.

Guide to meaning of terms

'*Immediate colleagues*', those you are accountable for (manager to team) or those in your immediate team (team member to team member).

'*To develop*', to facilitate a person having a changed opinion, view or level of knowledge or skill.

Comments and actions

Please add extra sheets if you need more space for your notes.

Comments

Actions

To be completed during your discussions with your supporter.

Negotiating with others

The ability to take into account the interests of both parties in order to gain a mutually satisfying outcome.

1. I see no opportunity for any negotiating my work situation.

2. I see some opportunities, but do not take advantage of them.

3. I attempt to negotiate at times but without confidence, due to lack of skills.

4. I have some skills in negotiating but lack the confidence in myself to use them at work.

5. I can negotiate in difficult situations* as long as it is only to try to influence* not to persuade.*

6. I can sometimes negotiate in difficult situations where I need to persuade the other party to accept my view.

7. I am confident about negotiating when the need arises and generally achieve my needs.

8. I attempt to negotiate to achieve the most mutually satisfying results for all parties, even in difficult situations.

9. The collaborative* negotiating style has become a natural part of my approach for achieving the best possible results for all parties, whatever the situation.

Please remember you may score between the numbers.

Space is provided for you to make comments to describe your personal level of effectiveness. You may find it useful to make notes as this might assist you in your discussion with your supporter.

Guide to meaning of terms

'*Difficult situations*', situations where you might feel pressured or threatened.

'*Influence*', an intention to help others to see your point of view, hoping they may decide to alter their view. There is no pressure on you.

'*Persuade*', you need to get others to accept your views against their initial opposition. There is pressure to succeed.

'*Collaborative*', working to hear and understand others' views to reach mutually satisfying results.

Comments and actions

Please add extra sheets if you need more space for your notes.

Comments

Actions

To be completed during your discussions with your supporter.

Honesty

The extent to which you communicate truthfully and sincerely.

1. I don't recognise the importance of giving honest* information and feedback.

2. While I recognise the importance, I have a strong tendency to avoid giving honest feedback or information.

3. Generally, I give honest feedback and information but on occasions I may withhold it even in relatively safe* situations.

4. Generally, I give honest information and feedback but I tend to withhold honest information which might be difficult to give and/or receive.

5. I am comfortable giving difficult and honest information and feedback to those with whom I feel safe.

6. I am uncomfortable but nearly always give difficult and honest feedback/information to those with whom I feel less safe.

7. I am confident and nearly always give difficult and honest feedback/information to those with whom I feel less safe.

8. In most situations before giving difficult and honest feedback/information, I think about the most effective approach. I do this within the constraints of personal and organisational safety.

9. In all situations I use the most effective method* to give difficult and honest feedback/information. I do so confidently as long as it is within the constraints of personal and organisational safety.*

Please remember you may score between the numbers.

Space is provided for you to make comments to describe your personal level of effectiveness. You may find it useful to make notes as this might assist you in your discussions with your supporter.

Guide to meaning of terms

'Honest', truthful and genuine.

'Safe', you feel that you will not be criticised, blamed or attacked. You do not perceive there to be any threat to your wellbeing.

'Effective method', judging what information to give in what style and when.

'Personal and organisational safety', not offending or putting ourselves, or others, or the organisation, at risk.

Comments and actions

Please add extra sheets if you need more space for notes.

Comments

Actions

To be completed during your discussions with your supporter.

Being articulate

The ability to express thoughts and ideas clearly in a way that enables others to understand fully the intended meaning.

1. Generally, I have difficulty saying what I mean.

2. I can say what I mean about familiar subjects* to those I know well.

3. I can say what I mean about familiar subjects to most people I talk to.

4. I express myself well to everyone when I am talking about familiar issues.*

5. I express myself confidently to everyone, even when I am talking about less familiar issues.

6. I express myself confidently when talking about issues which may be difficult for others to understand.

7. I am confident about finding effective ways to help others understand difficult or complex issues.*

8. I am confident about expressing myself clearly to others even when in uncomfortable or difficult situations.*

9. No matter how difficult the situation or complex the issue, I always express myself confidently in a way which clearly indicates what I mean and is easily understood by others.

Please remember you may score between the numbers.

Space is provided for you to make comments to describe your personal level of effectiveness. You may find it useful to make notes as this might assist you in your discussions with your supporter.

Guide to meaning of terms

'*Familiar subjects/issues*', having a good knowledge of the topic. You would be comfortable talking about this topic.

'*Difficult or complex issues*', no right or wrong answer, many different views involved.

'*Difficult situations*', situations where you might feel pressured or threatened.

Comments and actions

Please add extra sheets if you need more space for notes.

Comments

Actions

To be completed during your discussions with your supporter.

Creating relationships with others

The ability to develop effective working relationships which lead to productive outcomes.

1. I see no benefit in spending time and effort creating working relationships in the workplace.

2. I recognise the benefits in creating working relationships with colleagues.

3. I have difficulties in attempting to create working relationships with colleagues.

4. I create only a superficial relationship* with others at work.*

5. I create good working relationships but generally only with those with whom I immediately feel comfortable.

6. I am able to create effective working relationships with some people whom I initially find difficult or challenging.

7. I make an effort to create effective working relationships with even the most challenging of people.

8. If not immediately successful, I tend to persevere in creating effective working relationships, even with people I judge to be difficult.

9. I am good at judging and creating the most productive working relationship with all those with whom I come into contact at work.

10. I actively seek and create the most productive working relationship with others. This is regardless of my personal perception of the individual or whether they are a colleague or client.

Please remember you may score between the numbers.

Space is provided for you to make comments to describe your personal level of effectiveness. You may find it useful to make notes as this might assist you in your discussions with your supporter.

Guide to meaning of terms

'*Superficial relationship*', a surface-level relationship lacking depth and understanding of the individual.

'*Others at work*', this has a wider meaning than just colleagues, implying any person with whom you come into contact at work.

Comments and actions

Please add extra sheets if you need more space for notes.

Comments

Actions

To be completed during your discussions with your supporter.

Seeking true understanding

Striving for greater effectiveness, through a commitment to gain true and full understanding of any situation.

1. I recognise the importance of understanding things that affect my work.

2. If I do not understand and it seems safe,* I may ask questions or find other ways of seeking information.

3. I feel comfortable* asking questions and seeking information in most situations.

4. If it seems important, I can fully investigate situations even if I feel uncomfortable doing so.

5. I usually gather enough information to be able to work effectively.

6. I am able to analyse and make judgments using information gathered.

7. I feel confident and committed to gain a better understanding in complex and difficult situations.

8. In most situations I will work to gain a true and full understanding to increase effectiveness.

9. In every situation I will work to gain a true and full understanding to ensure maximum effectiveness.

Please remember you may score between the numbers.

Space is provided for you to make comments to describe your personal level of effectiveness. You may find it useful to make notes as this might assist you in your discussions with your supporter.

Guide to meaning of terms

'*Safe*', you feel that you will not be criticised, blamed or attacked as a result of asking any questions. You do not perceive there to be any threat to your wellbeing.

'*Comfortable*', you do not feel threatened in any way by the situation or the people to whom you are talking.

Comments and actions

Please add extra sheets if you need more space for notes.

Comments

Actions

To be completed during your discussions with your supporter.

Being responsible

Having an attitude in which you see that you are part of a larger whole, and that your duty extends to the care of that whole.

1. In everyday work situations I can act on my own initiative.*

2. When faced with an unusual* work situation, I can act on my own initiative where I feel confident.

3. When faced with an unusual work situation where I feel lacking in knowledge and confidence, I will only act in consultation with others.

4. When faced with an unusual work situation I am prepared to be responsible and work on my own initiative regardless of my knowledge and confidence. I may have difficult in accepting the consequences,* and occasionally may blame others.

5. When faced with an unusual work situation I am prepared to be responsible and work on my own initiative regardless of my knowledge and confidence. I am able to accept the consequences.

6. I am always prepared to be responsible, regardless of the situation. I may consider whether this is the responsibility of another, but I tend to take on the responsibility personally, and accept the consequences.

7. I am always prepared to be responsible regardless of the situation. I will consider whether to take personal responsibility or whether it is more appropriate for another person to take responsibility. I am able to 'let go' and accept the consequences.

8. I am committed to taking appropriate responsibility* in every work situation, and developing a work culture

where everyone is confident and comfortable to take full responsibility and accept the consequences.

9. I have the ability to judge for myself whether or not to be responsible in every situation, and I am prepared to accept the consequences. I work consistently to encourage this ability in others.

Please remember you may score between the numbers.

Space is provided for you to make comments to describe your personal level of effectiveness. You may find it useful to make notes as this might assist you in your discussions with your supporter.

Guide to meaning of terms

'*Initiative*', working independently, without consulting others.

'*Unusual*', a situation that arises at work, which is not a regular occurrence, and may be beyond your normal level of responsibility.

'*Accepting the consequences*', to be comfortable with the outcome and not to blame others in the event of error.

Comments and actions

Please add extra sheets if you need more space for notes.

Comments

Actions

To be completed during your discussions with your supporter.

Advising others

Recommending the appropriate course of action or development* to others.

Important: When reading these statements, advice is considered to be a positive skill.

1. I would not tell anyone how to do anything at work.

2. I have the opportunity to tell people how to do things at work, but tend to avoid doing so, because I am not confident.

3. I can tell people I am comfortable with how I believe they should do things.

4. I can tell people I am uncomfortable with how I believe they should do things.

5. I am confident about making recommendations to others in all areas where I feel knowledgeable.

6. I am confident about making recommendations to others in all areas where I feel knowledgeable and I can question to check out others' understanding.

7. I am confident about making recommendations to others in all areas where I feel knowledgeable. I can also use other skills to help people take on responsibility for their own development.*

8. I will consider the options for facilitating development in others and will knowingly choose advice when I consider it is the most comfortable option for myself.

9. I will knowingly choose advice when it is the most appropriate option for others.

10. When choosing the option of advice, I will work towards others taking on responsibility for their development.

Please remember you may score between the numbers.

Space is provided for you to make comments to describe your personal level of effectiveness. You may find it useful to make notes as this might assist you in your discussions with your supporter.

Guide to meaning of terms

'*Development*', where a person will have a changed opinion, view or level of knowledge or skill.

Comments and actions

Please add extra sheets if you need more space for notes.

Comments

Actions

To be completed during your discussions with your supporter.

Dealing with breakdowns

Extent to which you work through impenetrable situations which block progress.

1. I do not recognise breakdowns* at work in my work situation.

2. I recognise 'breakdowns' at work but feel I have no responsibility to do anything about them.

3. Although I recognise 'breakdowns' I dislike and avoid them.

4. I accept I have a responsibility but don't know how to work on the 'breakdowns'.

5. I know I have support from others should I choose to work through 'breakdowns'.

6. With the support of others, I work through 'break downs' towards progress.

7. In many situations I am able to work through 'breakdowns' using my own initiative.

8. I am able to work through most 'breakdowns' except when blocked by others.

9. Despite blockages from others* I am able to work through 'breakdowns'.

10. I am able to work through 'breakdowns' regardless of complexity and opposition. I also motivate and support others in working through 'breakdowns'.

Please remember you may score between the numbers.

Space is provided for you to make comments to describe your personal level of effectiveness. You may find it useful to make notes as this might assist you in your discussions with your supporter.

Guide to meaning of terms

'*Breakdowns*', impenetrable situations/problems at work which block progress (like hitting a brick wall).

'*Blockages from others*', people not prepared to accept responsibility. People deliberately being obstructive. People not committed to seeking an outcome etc.

Comments and actions

Please add extra sheets if you need more space for notes.

Comments

Actions

To be completed during your discussions with your supporter.

Trust at work

Having belief in the ability of other people and in yourself, to achieve the best possible results.

1. I have difficulty in trusting most people at work to do their job properly.

2. I am comfortable trusting the people I know well to do their job properly.

3. I trust the people I know at work, but have sometimes experienced regret* in my trust.

4. I am able to trust people I know at work, as long as they have not previously demonstrated a lack of ability.

5. I am comfortable trusting the people I know at work, regardless of the potential outcome.

6. I am comfortable trusting those I perceive to be trustworthy.* I believe in the importance of demonstrating trust in others and I consciously work towards developing others' trust in me.

7. I am comfortable trusting others, and believe in the importance of giving people opportunities to demonstrate trust.* I believe I am considered to be trustworthy in most circumstances.

8. I feel I am trustworthy and strongly believe in trusting others. I always work to encourage other to feel trusted.

9. I am comfortable demonstrating trust in everyone at work whom I believe to be trustworthy, regardless of potential outcome.* I believe I am trustworthy.

Please remember you may score between the numbers.

Space is provided for you to make comments to describe your personal level of effectiveness. You may find it useful to make notes as this might assist you in your discussions with your supporter.

Guide to meaning of terms

'*Experienced regret*', wishing that you had not trusted the person to do the work and would probably have preferred to do it yourself.

'*Trustworthy*', strives to be honest and open at all times.

'*Opportunities to demonstrate trust*', this may be taking a risk.

'*Regardless of the potential outcome*', letting go of control and feeling comfortable with either a positive/negative outcome.

Comments and actions

Please add extra sheets if you need more space for notes.

Comments

Actions

To be completed during your discussions with your supporter.

Creating the future

The extent to which you are prepared to work creatively towards meeting the challenges of an ever-changing future.

1. I am concerned only with the present work situation.

2. I sometimes think about how things might be different.*

3. I sometimes talk to others about doing things differently at work.

4. I try to operate creatively* to lead to a new way of doing things.

5. I constantly look for and make opportunities* to work creatively with others.

6. I am unorthodox* in the way in which I approach future opportunities at work.

7. I encourage others to join me in finding unorthodox ways of developing future opportunities for working together.

8. I am not afraid of promoting revolutionary approaches* to meeting the challenges of an ever-changing future.

9. Regardless of day-to-day pressure, I constantly explore different and revolutionary approaches to meeting the challenges of an ever-changing future.

Please remember you may score between the numbers.

Space is provided for you to make comments to describe your personal level of effectiveness. You may find it useful to make notes as this might assist you in your discussions with your supporter.

Guide to meaning of terms

'*Different*', a simple change which does not involve a major upheaval.

'*Creative(ly)*', freedom to think in alternative ways.

'*Opportunities*', a chance.

'*Unorthodox approaches*', operating with disregard to the normal.

Comments and actions

Please add extra sheets if you need more space for notes.

Comments

Actions

To be completed during your discussions with your supporter.

Completing the Personal Evaluation Wheel

When you have selected your ability level in each 'area', plot your scores on the Personal Evaluation Wheel (Figure 9.1).

The 'spokes' of the wheel shown here represent the 12 ability areas you have just scored. Match your score on the appropriate spoke for each area and mark with a cross. If you have chosen a mid-point between two numbers, put your cross between the two.

When you have completed all 12 spokes, join up the crosses with a pencil and ruler moving clockwise to each following spoke. Is there anything about the resulting

Figure 9.1 The Personal Evaluation Wheel

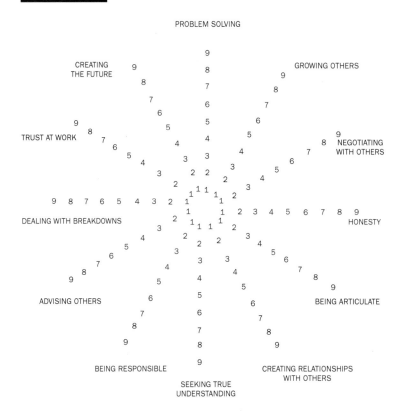

pattern that strikes you? If you think there is anything significant talk it over with your supporter or line manager.

Personal stock-take

By completing a personal stock-take, you will be reflecting on *how* you got to *where* you are today.

The personal stock-take asks a series of key questions to prompt self-reflection and to find out where you want to be in the future, in relation to your training and development career.

Taking stock of yourself requires you to be honest about yourself, your skills, knowledge and experience, both personal and professional. You will find it helpful to reflect on critical incidents as you answer the questions. While it covers educational and employment achievements, please include any outside work activities as well.

Choose a layout and format you like or design your own personal stock-take sheet. Questions to consider are listed below.

- Where am I at present in my personal and professional life?

- How did I get there?

- What educational achievements have I gained?

- What training and development have I successfully completed?

- What are my hobbies, interest and voluntary activities?

- What are my personal accomplishments? (Be fair to yourself!)

- What successes have I achieved at work?

- Who assisted me?

- What learning patterns have emerged?

- Where do I want to be...?
- What are my long-term ambitions/objectives?
- What skills and knowledge will I need to develop to attain my goals?
- How will it feel when I achieve my objectives?
- What things have I got going for me?
- What things are in my way?
- What concrete initiatives do I now need to take?
- What support will I need and from whom?

You may also find a SWOT analysis useful. This requires you to assess your

- strengths
- weaknesses
- opportunities
- threats

You may wish to supplement your SWOT answers with a PEST analysis. What are your learning needs here?

- political
- environmental
- social
- technological

For your first action plan, consider the following questions:

- What do I want to do?
- Why do I want to do this?
- What do I hope this piece of work will achieve?
- How will I know when I'm getting there?

10

The Strategic Evaluation Loop© and sample development plans

Identify strategic objectives

All organisations have strategic objectives. These are the high-level aims that the board have targeted to grow and build the business. They are usually reviewed every five years or so and are often broken down further into department objectives, team targets and individual goals. It should be readily apparent that there is a link between all of these, not unlike an audit trail. Some examples of strategic objectives are:

- increase market share by 20 per cent over the next five years;
- develop knowledge management of staff to retain market leadership status;
- migrate into new markets in Asia;
- build a reliable IT infrastructure.

Department objectives usually involve internal customer/ supplier service agreements. Team targets are usually aimed at outputs especially in relation to time, cost and quality.

Figure 10.1 Strategic Evaluation Loop©

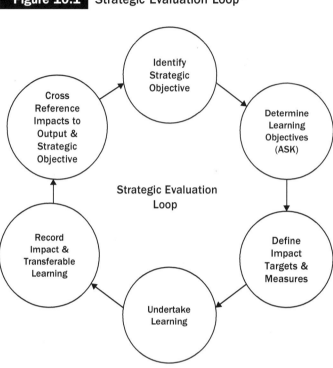

Individual goals should be split 65/35 into outputs/learning growth.

Determine learning objectives (ASK)

To be effective, any learning needs to be targeted. Identifying what you are trying to learn or change is critical to the process. This can easily be broken down further into:

- *Attitude*: This can easily be explained by adopting the aeronautical definition. Attitude is defined as the angle of approach that an aeroplane has toward the earth. An incorrect attitude has an immediate impact on effectiveness.

Is the learning objective to alter the angle of approach that the learner has towards something?

- *Skills*: This is best looked at from the point of view of deploying the skills in an appropriate way to ensure that the task is achieved. How does the learner do this at the moment? Are they competently deploying the skills? Are they confident in their deployment?

- *Knowledge*: This looks at the learner's underpinning knowledge. A good way to look at this is to ask whether they have enough knowledge to teach another the theory and the practical application of something. Just having the practical application is not enough to ensure growth of knowledge and best practice.

Once this is determined and discussed with the learner and the tutor/coach/mentor, the next stage can be undertaken.

Define impact targets and objective

So far the process has concerned itself with both the bigger picture and the outcomes. However, for effective evaluation of coaching or mentoring we have to look at the impact rather than the outcomes. Coaching and mentoring are too far removed from the outcomes to honestly say that that they have made x amount of difference to y. If you coach someone on say, time management, and their next report comes in on time, there can be any number of other contributing factors – not least that someone important shouted for that report louder than anyone else! A better approach would be to say that if someone were coached on time management, what *impact* would that have on their planning and prioritisation techniques. There is a case here for having the coaching take place prior to attending any learning intervention.

Undertake learning

Once all of the above has taken place, the learning intervention can take place. Examples of such intervention include:

- coaching;
- mentoring;
- training course;
- secondment;
- work shadow;
- teaching others;
- exams;
- OJT qualifications;
- giving presentations;
- external talks;
- lectures;
- open learning;
- book reviews;
- interactive learning.

The above list is not exhaustive, but is designed to illustrate that there is more to a learning intervention that 'just another training course'.

Record impact and transferable learning

There are two very important aspects here. The first one is to record the impact that the learning intervention has had on the targeted areas. Depending on the diligence deployed in the earlier stages of this process, this should be relatively straightforward. Indeed most 'smile sheets' – the term used to describe the validation sheets that are used at the end of a training course – should have questions on them to assist this. The second area is one that is more often than not ignored or forgotten. Experience tells us that when someone learns something, they very often adopt and adapt the patterns they have learnt and deploy them in other areas. This is not however planned – but it should be. Engaging in a conversation that highlights where the learning could be transferred would not only be beneficial, but also prudent in terms of cost.

Take the earlier example of someone being coached on time management. Having already established that it has an impact on the learner's planning and prioritisation skills, we should then ask 'as well as workload management, where else could improved planning and prioritisation be of benefit?' or 'who else in the team could benefit from learning these techniques, that would improve either the department's outputs or the service you receive from them?'

Missing out on the second part of this conversation means that you will only get half of the benefit.

Cross-reference impacts to outputs and strategic objective

The final action in this process is to trace the impact of the learning intervention back to the original strategic objective. As mentioned previously, if the individual goals, team targets and departmental objectives are all 'joined up', this trail back to the strategic object almost looks after itself.

Like most evaluation processes, the final part gets missed off, forgotten, or people race onto the next project.

The easier the evaluation process is made, the less it costs. Given that evaluation costs money, there is undoubtedly a law of diminishing returns at work here.

The following are key to successful development plans:

- Be specific about what you're going to do.

- Set deadlines – both interim and completed.

- Make sure your plan is realistic in terms of what to accomplish and when.

- Schedule, and then carry out, periodical progressive checks.

- As much as possible, design your plan around things you want and like to do (if your development plan is just hard work, you'll find ways to avoid it).

- Plan ways to work on your skills and goals as part of your everyday routine, both at work and at home.

- Make your plan visible. Post it on the wall in front of you.

Development plan

Name	
Date	
No.	
For period (from/to)	
Development goal	
Where do I want to be?	
What do I want to be doing?	
How will I feel?	
What new knowledge and skills do I need?	
How will I achieve this?	
What resources/support do I need?	
What constraints do I foresee?	
What are my criteria for success?	
Target dates	

Personal development plan to identify CPD needs

Name	
Date	
No.	
My long-term goal(s)	
Personal aspirations	
Professional development need	
Organisational needs	
I have the following skills, knowledge and experience to help my development:	
Skills	
Knowledge	
Experience	
Short-term objectives	
Medium-term objectives	
Long-term objectives	
Summary of planned development activity	
What resources or support will I need?	
What are my success criteria?	

Learning contract

Objectives	
Actions	
Resources	
Target dates	
Signature	
Date	

11

Recording your CPD: learning log and development records

Learning log

Ironically, those who are least attracted to the idea, actually stand to gain the most from keeping a log.

What is a learning log?

A learning log allows the individual to record significant learning experiences that occur during everyday activity. By writing down 'what happened', 'what was learned' and 'what I would do differently in a similar situation in the future', there is every likelihood that things will be carried out better – with real learning having taken place.

Why keep a learning log?

Everyone is different and therefore the reasons and motivations for keeping a log will be many.

- Learning logs allow those individuals – activists – who flit from one activity to another without taking time to review how things were actually achieved to become more reflective in their approach.

- Learning logs will allow those individuals who are by nature reflectors/theorists to create action plans for new situations following reflection.

Completion of a learning log

The learning log included here contains prompts within the layout which you may find useful.

The first part of the log is about 'preparing for a given learning situation', while the second part helps to 'get the learning out'. The 'ponder session' might be a useful alternative.

Please feel free to devise a recording method of your own, if you prefer.

Learning log part I: preparation

The experience	
Preparation for the activity	
Where/when will it take place?	
What do I intend to gain from this activity?	
Who will be involved and what do I need from them?	
What might my approach be?	
What resources will I require?	
What preparation do I need to do?	

Learning log part II: getting the learning out

Describe how the activity went	
What were your learning experiences?	
Reflect on your input to the activity	
How did this learning experience relation to your CPD goal(s)?	
How will you use the learning?	
Any further action	

Ponder session

What was the purpose of the activity/meeting/experience?	
What have you learned?	
How could you apply what you have learned?	

Development review

Date:	
No:	
Long-term objective	
Where do I want to be?	
How do I want to live my life?	
What did I want/need to learn?	
What did I do to achieve this?	
What did I learn?	
How will I use it?	
Any further action?	
Target dates for review/completion	

Informal learning experiences

Learning experience	
How did I have this experience?	
What did I learn?	
How will I use it?	
Any future action?	

Development records

Further suggestions for learning opportunities you might like to record:

- reading reviews;
- meeting reports;
- coaching conversation reviews;
- mentoring meeting reviews;
- learning diary.

The preceding formats can be easily adapted to suit any of the above. Alternatively, devise your own using other media including sound and vision.

Personal statement

It is the aim of the personal statement to allow you to capture your unique style of working and learning:

- *Length*: about 200 words;
- *Content*: personal characteristics, your values, style, learning and work preferences.

Bibliography

Davidoff, S. and van den Berg, O. (1990) *Changing Your Teaching*, Johannesburg: Centaur Publications.

Driver, R. and Erickson, G. (1983) 'Theories-in-action: Some theoretical and empirical issues in the study of students' conceptual frameworks in science', *Studies in Science Education* 10: 37–60.

Downs, S. (1995) *Learning at Work: Effective Strategies for Making Learning Happen*, London: Kogan Page.

Ellis, R. (1985) *Understanding Second Language Acquisition*, Oxford: Oxford University Press.

Forrest, A. (1994) *5-Way Management*, London: Industrial Society.

Honey, P. and Mumford, A. (2006) *Learning Styles Questionnaire: 80-Item Version*, Maidenhead: Peter Honey Publications.

McCarthy, B. (1980) 'Learning styles applications', available at: *http://www.gp-training.net/training/educational_theory/ reflective_learning/learning_styles/lsq.htm* (accessed 17 July 2008).

Megginson, D. and Whitaker, V. (1996) *Cultivating Self Development Training Essentials*, London: CIPD Books.

Tidswell, K. and Rogers, K. (1998) *Practical Learning Styles*, Tidswell and Rogers: Oxford.

Verster, C. 'Learning styles and teaching', available at: *http://www.teachingenglish.org.uk/think/articles/learning-styles-teaching* (accessed 19 July 2008).

Index

12 ability areas, 48

accepting the consequences, 76
activists, 35
adventurers, 8
advice, 78–80
analytic learners, 41–2
articulate, 66–7
attitude, 94
auditory learning style, 40

Belbin's Team Role Inventory, 31
blockages from others, 82
breakdowns, 82
    dealing with, 81–3
building up contacts, 46

checklist scoring system, 23–4
Coaching Competencies
    Assessment Questionnaire, 31
collaborative, 61
commonsense learners, 42
complex problem, 55
concepts, 3–4
CPD:
    benefits of, 5–6
    portfolio, 19
    practical process, 4–5
    recording, 17
    supporting, 16
creative skills, 46

determine learning objectives
    (ASK), 94–5
develop others, 46
development checklist, 23–30
development plan, 15–16,
    93–101
development records, 103–7
development review, 106
difficult or complex issues, 67
difficult situations, 61, 67
doer – thinker, 33
duties, change of, 45
dynamic learners, 42

effective learning, 7–8
evaluation, discussion of, 49

familiar subjects/issues, 67
field-independent vs. field-
    dependent, 40, 43
future, creating the, 87–9

group work, 44
growing others, 57–9
guidance, respond to, 46

honesty, 63–5
Honey & Mumford's Learning
    Styles, 35–9
Honey & Mumford's Learning
    Styles Questionnaire, 31

immediate colleagues, 58
impact and transferable learning, 96–7
incidental learning, 7
individual learning, 44
industrial society, 44
influence, 61
informal learning experiences, 106
initiative, 76
innovative learners, 41
instructional preference, 33
interaction, 32
intuitive learning, 7

kinaesthetic learning style, 40
knowledge, 95

learner types of, 8
learning:
   and learning styles, 31–46
   as a planned activity, 8
   process, 7–11, 34
   sources of, 11
learning contract, 16, 101
learning cycle, 9
learning log, 17, 103–7
Learning Styles Questionnaire, 11
learning styles, 10–11
   guidance on, 38–9
learning types of, 7
left-brain vs. right-brain, 41, 43–4
line manager, 51

manage people, 26–8
manage your environment, 28–9
manage your job, 25–6
manage your specialist function, 30

manage yourself, 24
Margerison-McCann Team Management Development, 31
McCarthy's four learning styles, 41–2
mental representation, 34
MUD acronym, 9
Myers Briggs Type Indicator, 31

negotiation, 60–1
neurolinguistic programming, 39

orientation, 32
others at work, 70

personal and organisational safety, 64
personal development plan, 100
personal development, fifty ways, 44–6
Personal Evaluation Tool, 31, 47–92
   guidelines, 51–90
   purpose of, 47–8
Personal Evaluation Wheel, 49, 90–1
personal statement, 107
personal stock-take, 13–14, 91–2
persuade, 61
PEST analysis, 92
planned learning and emergent learning concepts of, 9
planning, 9
ponder session, 105
Practical Learning Styles, 32–3
Practical Learning Styles Questionnaire, 31
pragmatists, 38

preparations, 13–14
principles, 3
problem solving, 54–5
processing, 32
prospective learning, 7

realistic – creative, 33
reflectors, 37
representation, 32, 45
responsibility, 75–7
retrospective learning, 7
reviewing, 9

sages, 8
self-evaluation of ability areas,
    48–9
simple problem, 55
skills, 95
sleepers, 8
Strategic Evaluation Loop,
    93–101
strategic objective, 93–4, 97–8

study approach, 33
superficial relationship, 70
supporter, coach or mentor, 50
surface processor – deep
    processor, 34
SWOT analysis, 92

tactile way of learning, 40
targets and objective, 95–6
teaching, four modalities of,
    42–3
theorists, 37–8
trust at work, 84–7

understanding, 72–4
user, 50

verbaliser – visualiser, 34
visual learning style, 39–40

warriors, 8
working relationships, 69–71